# POEMS FOR HOW YOU FEEL

## By Chris Jones

© COPYRIGHT 2012, 2017 SEEJONES PUBLISHING

**By The Same Author**

**<u>Novel</u>**

**Flying On A Dream**
**Adult Fiction**
>   Adventure, Drama, Romance and Suspense.

This book embraces the strange dreams and hopes of a wealthy Japanese businessman.  Through his greed for power, he creates a human experiment that turns into a real life adventure in America.

**<u>Stories</u>**
**Adult and Children's fiction**
>   Adventure and Suspense.

**The Dark Side – The Rise of Zin**
**The Dark Side – The New World Order**
**The Dark Side – The Keeper of the Gate**

These series tell of a man determined to rule the world by creating two dimensions and a boy who will do everything to stop him.

**PLEASE VISIT MY WEBSITE & STORE**

**www.seejones.webnode.com**

*© COPYRIGHT 2012, 2017 SEEJONES PUBLISHING*

LEGAL NOTICE
All rights reserved. No part of this book may be
Reproduced, stored in a retrieval system, or transmitted in any
form, or by any means, electronic, mechanical, photocopying,
recording or otherwise, without prior written permission from the
Author, Chris Jones.

Chris Jones has asserted his right under Section 77 of the
Copyright, Designs and Patents Act 1988 to be identified as the
author of this work.

# POEMS

Have you ever read a poem and thought it was very nice, but you didn't quite get it?

Do you find that some poems are so mystical and would only mean something to the author?

Some poems are written in codes and you are expected to sit and ponder what the meanings could be. Some poets make their meaning so abstract that you lose interest straight away.

Well, you will not have that problem with this book of poetry. I have categorized and written an introduction to each poem.

I guarantee you will find at least 3 poems in this book that will hit you like a hammer and you will be able to identify with and relate to.


ENJOY!!!

# PREFACE

After being diagnosed with Parkinson's disease, having a stroke, Bells Palsy and just falling apart, I started to feel sorry for myself. I stopped eating, going out and attending any type of social functions. I slept all day and the only thing that I would do was attend medical appointments.

My family and friends watched me fall from a successful accountant, accomplished pianist and a fairly good singer with recordings still selling after many years. Now I'm a depressed sick person.

One day a friend visited me and brought a poem. I told my friend "I don't do poems. I can't understand them. I need to understand the things that I read." My friend ignored me and began to read a poem entitled, 'And Still I Rise' by Dr. Maya Angelou. I jumped out of the bed and I had to read it for myself, again…and again…

Later I heard a song on the radio. It was entitled 'Still I Rise' sung by Yolanda Adams. So I went out and purchased Dr. Maya Angelou's book and Yolanda Adams' CD.

Soon I started writing a collection of poems and decided to go all the way and publish them myself.

Thank you Dr. Maya Angelou

For all the magnificent things that you do
Your writing has inspired me
One who was going through

Thank you Dr. Maya Angelou
I had once given up on life
Now I'm doing things with a talent I never knew
I may fall down, but I'll get up
I now rise because of people just like you.

Thank you, Dr. Maya Angelou
I dedicate this book to you.

# TABLE OF CONTENTS

# CHAPTER ONE


## MARRIAGE

## *The Introduction*

NO, NOT TONIGHT

Have you ever experienced a relationship that was totally one-sided?  After a short while, all of the sweetness and attention became a thing of the past.  You still did things for that person just like in the beginning and yet you were not appreciated.

You were taken for granted and no consideration for your feelings was recognized.  That person seemed to do everything to belittle you and the relationship was far from equal. Yet and still that person demanded physical favors and you were expected to satisfy their needs when they wanted.

How selfish can a person be?

*The Poem*

## NO, NOT TONIGHT

My husband takes me for granted; you've heard this before
I serve him with pleasure, right from the front door

He never talks to me nor does he treat me right
So my answer to him is "No, not tonight!"

He wined and dined me in the beginning or the start
He now ignores me just like an old fart

He no longer tells me that I am pretty
He takes away my confidence and thinks that he is so witty

No new dresses for me; he always says that money is tight
So my answer to him is "No, not tonight!"

Where did it go?  The laughter and fun
The sweet little nicknames, like 'baby' and 'hun.'

I look at him now, a stranger I see
A person who lives in the same house with me

So, if he ever bothers to ask, because he thinks I might
My answers to him will be, "No, not tonight!"

# CHAPTER TWO

## *DEATH OF A LOVED ONE*

## *The Introduction*

DEAR MOTHER

Have you ever heard someone speak of their regrets for not being closer to their parents? They speak of not being there and being ungrateful for what they have been given.

They realize after the death, they never even said, "I love you."

They cry excessively at the funeral because of the guilt and the shame they feel.

I believe that loved ones should be given their flowers (thanks and praise) before they pass on.

I attended a funeral and the daughter of the deceased said that she had not spoken to her mother for almost a year. And now it was too late to tell her mother just how she feels.

*The Poem*

## DEAR MOTHER

Dear mother, you are now gone and I think of the things I didn't
say
Mother I love you so much, although you were set in your own
way

I did not share my feelings or tell you about any of my dreams
Still you always loved me, and ran to me whenever you heard the
screams

You held me in your arms and told me that all was okay
I never imagined that one-day, you would go away

You gave me all you had and never once complained
You worked your fingers to the bone and your body was totally
drained

I never said how much I appreciated all the things you did for me
And I never took the time…not even for a cup a tea

Dear mother, now you are gone and my tears are bubbling inside
I thank God for you mother and I do realize just how hard you
tried

## *The Introduction*

MY LITTLE FLOWER

My little flower is about my mother.  As she got older, I watched her wither away.

She accomplished much as far as I am concerned.  She raised me and my siblings the best that she could, and she gave us love as best as a mother could.

## LITTLE FLOWER

My little flower
No sunshine, no rain
Poor little flower in so much pain

The pedals are dropping, one by one
It won't be long before its day is done

The leaves are dried and are wilting away
The stem was once strong and straight; everything was okay

The root was once stable and secure
Buried in the warm soil, so rich and so pure

God has taken my loving mother so she will suffer no more
And I know that she is standing, right at heaven's door

My little flower has gone away
But the memories of her, will always stay

# CHAPTER THREE

## *LONELINESS*

## *The Introduction*

I'VE NEVER BEEN IN LOVE

One day while riding on a train for a long journey, I met a woman that really impressed me with her vast accomplishments.

This person was well traveled and versed on many subjects.  She had experienced so many things that the normal person could not even fathom.

But when I began talking about my relationships and family, she had nothing to say.  I then realized that she was very lonely and although she had been there, done this and that, there was one thing that she had never experienced.  She had never been in love.

*The Poem*

## I'VE NEVER BEEN IN LOVE

I've been to the ocean and I've crossed many seas
I've studied the nature of the birds and the bees

I talked to a man who said he's been to the moon
I've been in a place where they don't work afternoon

I've been on an island where the day never ends
I've been in a race where no one ever wins

I could write a big book and tell you of many things
Talk about hope and tell you all of my dreams
But there is one special thing that I'm missing above…I've never
been in love.

I've sipped from a cup made of silver and gold
I've stayed in a house that was five hundred years old

I've watched as the sand slowly tick away time
I've been on a mountain that no one could ever climb

I've been on a desert where it rains once a year
I've been in a place filled with hatred and fear

But there is one special thing that I'm missing above…I've never
been in love

# CHAPTER FOUR

## *DEPRESSION*

*** **The Introduction**

DEPRESSION

Everyone experiences depression at one time or another. Some people fall into a lingering depression. You stay in the bed. You don't eat. All you want to do is sleep.

You feel that you are worthless and your life is incomplete. You forget about all the things that you should be thankful for.

My grandmother use to tell me about the man that was so sad because he had no shoes. He complained until he met a man with no feet.

If everything were just as you wanted it to be, you would not appreciate anything.

So what you've experienced setbacks. If not for those bad days, how would you know when you are having a good day?

## DEPRESSION

I laid down to rest
Why?  Because I am so depressed
I sleep from dusk to dawn
Only to awake and think of the things that has gone wrong

My body is weak, and yet I can't be bothered to eat
My spirit is low and my faith has lost its glow
My physical appearance has grown shallow and frail
And all of my failures of the past begin to tell a tale

The groans from my belly are now short and quake
How much of this cruel world can I take?

But if I am never depressed
How can I tell the bad times from the best?

And so I must get up and eat
I must take charge of my life and stand to my feet

For God's intention is not for me to be depressed
For he only wants me, to be blessed

PERSONALITY

Sometimes in many lives, feelings of despair occur. Sometimes it leads to severe depression and hopelessness. In some situations, this disparity can lead to feelings of self-harm and in some cases, suicide. In these moments, it is good to talk to someone. That someone can even be a stranger.

It's good to remember that everyone is someone in this world. Everyone contributes something in his or her lifetime. No matter how small and insignificant you feel, you help to make up this world.

***The Poem***

**PERSONALITY**

Yesterday I sat down and had a talk with my friend
I told him that my life was boring and I just want it to end

He said, "You got personality.  I got personality."

He said I got so much to live for
And there ain't nothing in this world to die for

I took a ride in my car where the river bends
I asked myself as I cried, should I drive right in?
Then I heard a voice say "Don't you give in."

It said that if you give up, you'd never see the light
It ain't a war, it ain't a crime, it's just a simple fight…but you
can win.

So never give up
Never give in

Because you got personality

# CHAPTER FIVE

## DEALING WITH DISABILTIES

*The Introduction*

DISABLED CHILD

One day I visited a Children's Hospital.  A friend of mine had just given birth. Unfortunately, her child arrived early and was kept for observation.

As I sat and looked around, the waiting room was filled with disabled children suffering from many different deformities.

I began to wonder, why has God let these children suffer so much?  What a difficult time the parents will have.

One thing that caught my attention was all of the children had smiles on their faces, just happy to be alive.

I then began to realize that these children are examples of what I could have been. And I believe that they are blessed beyond my understanding.  Their conditions are there for me to see. And if it had not been for the grace of God, there would be me.

## DISABLED CHILD

My poor disabled child
I told myself it was only for a while

I'd pray each morning when I awake, that by some miracle,
This disability of my child, the Lord will take

I curse each night before I sleep, why didn't you show up God?
Not even one peep

I cried and screamed out 'Why God, Why?'
If you won't help my child, then let him die!

He is unable to walk, talk or fend for his own
He tries to smile although he suffers with pain down to the bone

How could you let him agonize so much?
When only from you, it would take just one touch

The truth that I had to learn,
Is that although he is flesh of my flesh and bone of my bones,
His soul belongs to God and is not my own

If his disability is an example of what I could be
Then I know that in heaven, he will be free

He'll run, sing and play each and every day
But for my sake, God made him this way

# CHAPTER SIX

# DEALING WITH FAMILY

## *The Introduction*

FAMILY REUNION

It is becoming more and more popular for families to have reunions.

Everyone has one of those T-Shirts commemorating the date of this joyous occasion. People travel from near and far to attend.

The same issues are similar in most families. There is the drunken uncle, and the master of the grill forbidding anyone to come near. The old folks telling stories of 'In my day.' The people eating most of the food are those who are not even related. And then there's the big argument that no one knows how it was started.

I do love family reunions!

## FAMILY REUNION

Once a year, we'd all gather together
We'd cook on the grill, no matter the weather

Aunts and uncles, brothers and sisters
Even the man from across the alley; the kids call mister

The music blasting from the stereo surround
Uncle Bubba is drunk and nowhere to be found

Grandmother would tell stories of how it was in the past
Grandfather would mumble and call her a pain in the …

Little cousin Ernie would dirty his clothes
And his big brother Joey, would just sit and pick his nose

We'd all have on t-shirts to remember the date
When the family gathered together, even the ones we sometimes
hate

# CHAPTER SEVEN

## COPING WITH FRIENDS

FRIENDS

We all have people in our lives that we call friends.  You know, those people that borrow money, your clothes, your car, your lawn mower and on, and on.

Why must we have friends?  They hurt your feelings, betray you, gossip about you and smile in your face.

How many of these so called friends can you honestly say will never desert you?

I can't think of any.  Can you?

## FRIENDS

Why do friends think nothing to borrow your money?
They think even less to pay you back
Why do friends laugh and talk about you, only to hide the things
they lack

Why do friends borrow your things and get angry because you
asked for them to be returned?
And when you need a favor from them, they never do it but yet
act so concerned

Why do friends stand on your back to lift themselves up?
Only to look down at you, like you are a beggar with a cup

Why do friends tell you that they care so much about you and
your welfare?
And when you need them the most, it's so obvious they really
don't care

Why do friends love to gossip and spread vicious rumors?
And if you don't conspire with them, they call you mean and
don't possess a sense of humor

There is only one friend I have that doesn't treat me this way
I can put my trust in him and he is there each and every day

I can go without my so-called friends because they're not very
nice
Thank you to all my pretend friends
The next time you ask me for something, I'll think twice

# CHAPTER EIGHT

*HOPEFUL*

## *The Introduction*

NEW YEAR

Every New Year I set my goals with a better vision.  I try to get rid of all those things that use to keep me down.  I try to change habits and the old tired people that hang around.

I want to make better choices and stick to a plan.  I want to feel better about myself and have new things to look forward to.

Every New Year I try to introduce to myself a brand new me and not get back into the same old rut.

Maybe this New Year, I will have better luck.

## NEW YEAR

Here it is, a brand new year
Setting new goals
I only have myself to fear

I have new desires and new concerns
No longer putting others first
It's a New Year and its now my turn

The old year has passed and some relationships have gone
I'm going to put my chin up and welcome in a new dawn

Friends of new and friends of old
There will be new stories and lies to be told

It's a brand new year
I can't change the past
Will it be a new relationship, or marriage and will it last

New hopes and new visions I will try to set into stone
I'm smiling in delight, I don't know why, because I'm still all
alone

It's another new year and to myself, I will make this note
I will not spend another year,
In love with another old goat

# CHAPTER NINE

## *RELATIONSHIPS*

IF I WOULD'VE, COULD'VE, SHOULD'VE

Sometime in many lives, feelings of regret occur.  Mostly in failed relationships there are feelings of 'If I had the chance to do it over again.'

For many years, I have felt this way about a special person.  I thought the grass was greener with someone else, and it wasn't.  I let that person get away. And until I die, I will never stop regretting my choice.

Only if I would've, could've and should've.

*The Poem*

# IF I WOULD'VE, COULD'VE, SHOULD'VE

If I would've been more understanding, I would not be alone
If I could've been more forgiving,
I would have given more love than I had shown
I should've seen your love for me and how much it has grown

If I would've paid more attention to you, and not want
everything my way
I could've listened to you more, and not push you farther away
I should've have spent more time with you; more than a few
hours a day

If I would've told you just how much I loved you,
I could've stopped you from leaving and saying that we're
through
I should've seen that your love for me was honest, good and true

If I would've, could've, should've realized just how much you
meant to me
And if I had just one more chance,
I'd love you endlessly

SO GLAD

At last, my love has come along.  Sometimes it takes years to find someone to love you unconditionally. Someone that believes in you and supports all that you do.  They are there to pick you up when you are down and know just what to say to bring you around.  They share in your sorrows, grief, and losses and are proud of all your accomplishments.  Many times we forget to let them know how grateful and appreciative we are.

So when you find this person, never take them for granted.

*The Poem*

## SO GLAD

It took some time for me to understand
A true love is so hard to find
I will never take your love for granted
Because you are and will for forever, stay on my mind

I am so glad that you see in me what I can be
I'm so glad that you are in my life
I am so glad that you believe in me and only me
I'm so glad that you're mine

With every moment that I'm with you each day
Every second that we spend of our lives
We'll chase the sorrows into tomorrows
And wash our fears away
And our love will be new every day

You've no idea the inspiration that you bring to me
And to know that it's real
Not just a fling
Not just a thrill
This thing that we have is for real

I am so glad that you're mine.

# CHAPTER TEN

## *SPIRITUALLY SPEAKING*

## *The Introduction*

HE IS REAL

At one time, I was a Doubting Thomas.  I had many friends that also shared the same questions about God.

One day I was sitting in the garden and I watched nature at its finest.  There was a bird that flew down and dug up a worm from the dirt.  How did that bird know that there was a worm there?

I looked on the ground and I saw an ant carrying a piece of bread twice its size.  How did that ant do it?

I saw a bee entering a flower.  How did that bee know to do that?

The sun was out and shining very bright.  Why didn't it fall down to the earth?

Then I really got clever.  I thought about lions and tigers and their prey.  Predators have an advantage over deer and such prey because of their strength.  Then I had an epiphany; predators have eyes in the front of their faces while the prey is given something different that somewhat evens the stakes a little.  The prey has eyes on the sides of their faces, hence giving the ability to see more of an area.

I started to think of things that I took for granted.  Hey, these things could not have happen so perfectly by chance and I concluded that God is definitely real!

*The Poem*

## HE IS REAL

One night I meditated and sat very still
I wanted to know for once and for all, is He real?

I searched very deep into my past
And why the good times never last

I can clearly remember all the bad times that I have endured
And I always ended up calling on the Lord

There were times that I refused to believe
Surely a God like this would not leave me to grieve

The pains and trouble that He…No I put me through
Just a simple prayer, no that won't do

Now I see things differently through brand new eyes
And I now can see through all of those lies

That old satan whispered into my ear
Your Lord and God doesn't really care

Now I am singing a brand new song
And I know for sure that satan is very wrong

Now I am stronger and no longer bound
Because I know that God is always around

And I know just what I feel
Yes I know, He is truly real!

## *The Introduction*

I FORGIVE ME

So many times we are told to ask God for forgiveness. We cry and pray and the Bible tells us that God answers our prayers.

Well, I believe that this is true. But there's something that we neglect to do; forgive ourselves. We hold on to old memories filled with guilt and persecution. We carry these things most of our lives and allow them to bring us down. These past transgressions become additional weight in our hearts and minds.

We must accept the fact that God's word is true.

So let's forgive ourselves.

God already has.

*The Poem*

**I FORGIVE ME**

I forgive me for the wrong things that I have done
For treating people unkind and having compassion for none

I forgive me for thinking I was better than others
Not willing to lend a hand to my sisters and brothers

I forgive me for hating those blessed with prosperity
When many times they have come to my aid and I treated them
horribly

I forgive me for not helping those I could
And because of my selflessness, I meant them no good

I forgive me for all my thoughts of lust and desire
I brought people down just to lift myself higher

I forgive me for all the guilt's of the past
And causing others hurt that will forever last

Now it is time for me to set my mind and heart free
I have prayed to God to help me to be all that He wants me to be

And because He loves me so much,
He has already forgiven me.

# CHAPTER ELEVEN

## *BETRAYAL*

*The Introduction*

IF YOU'RE LONELY, YOU'RE NOT A FRIEND OF MINE

I wrote this to help comfort myself after being betrayed by someone that I thought was my friend.

I was engaged to be married and thought that my fiancé was heaven sent.
I was so much in love; I could never imagine that my match made in heaven would turn to hell.

You see, I had a friend; no, I thought I had a friend that was very lonely and I thought loyal.
I would take this so-called friend with me to my fiancé's home and we would have diner and occasionally take in a movie.

One night I came home unexpected just for a surprise. However, it was me that was surprised. I caught my fiancé and my "friend" together. Well you can imagine the rest.

Keep away from lonely people.

*The Poem*

## IF YOU'RE LONELY YOU'RE NOT A FRIEND OF MINE

Compromising situations sometimes can lead to a whole lot more
You just start out with some friendly talk
And it leads you to the bedroom door

I can only speak for myself, and all that I have been through
Lonely people don't make good friends because they'll take
advantage of you

People tell me, that you are just using me
You come to my house when you know I'm not home
Taking liberties with no respect for me
Lonely people can have hearts of stone

So if you're lonely, you're not a friend of mine
If you're lonely, you don't have peace of mind

# CHAPTER TWELVE

## *REJECTION*

*The Introduction*

IS THERE A PLACE IN YOUR HEART FOR ME

Have you ever been in love with someone and you felt that you were driving on a one-way street?

Have you ever felt a longing to be with someone, but your feelings were not shared?

All you needed to do was to ask, "Am I wasting my time?"

## IS THERE A PLACE IN YOUR HEART FOR ME

Innocent dreams, stealing my heart away
I can't decide which is night, which is day

Only to awake with you on my mind
I'm searching for a love that I will never find

I wish you could feel this emptiness inside
It hurts so much; all I can do is cry

Knowing that your love is so far away
Yet I feel you near me, what a price to pay

Biding my time on an endless case
Longing for that smile upon your face

I can't just wait day to day
I'm spending my life just dreaming away

Why am I so much in love with you?
You touched my spirit and my heart too

I can't go on fooling myself
Trying to fall in love with someone else

Is there a place in your heart for me?
Or is it just an empty room?

# CHAPTER THIRTEEN

## *MOTIVATIONAL*

NOT GOING MY WAY

Are you the type of person that gives 100% to each project that you take on?  You get knocked down but you always get up and keep on trying.

Does it seem that all of your endeavors fail to pan out and you feel hopeless?  Does it appear to you that others accomplish their goals without trying?  Or others seem to have good fortunes drop in their laps even when they don't deserve it.  Does your life appear to go around in circles with no end or satisfaction?

I believe that one should never give up trying and persevere no matter what.  After all you should be happy for what you have and remember that there are others much worse off than you are.

*The Poem*

**Not Going My Way**

How do I keep myself going when everything seems to always
go wrong?
How do I make myself feel good when the torment seems so
long?

I wonder if in this world, is it possible to be strong
I try not to give up, but it's still the same old song

Surely I can't be the only one that feels this pain
If it's not me, then who is to blame

I give my best effort in all that I try
But with each failed endeavor, I still cry

Do I have the right to complain?
When there are people that only wish for rain

Their stomachs are empty and their futures are so bleak
They walk for miles just for something to eat

Cries go unheard and their spirits are weak
But yet I pity myself because I feel so incomplete

I constantly complain and cry the blues
When there are people who wish that they were in my shoes

I have so much to be thankful for each and every day
Although things are not…going my way.

*The Introduction*

OLD BLIND MAN

Everyday on my way to work, I'd passed by this older gentleman.  He was blind but he always knew when I was passing by.

This old blind man was very articulate with his greeting and his appearance was always impeccable. Some mornings I would apply different perfumes, but he still knew that it was me. Some mornings I would change my walking habits by walking soft and sometimes heavy.  Still he always knew it was me.

I started to believe that he was not blind but pretended to be.  One day I saw him with his wife and he held her arm for guidance. To me, this confirmed that he was truly blind.

Seeing is a blessing and all of the wonderful things in life we ignore and miss. Could it be that in some ways, we are blind.

*The Poem*

## OLD BLIND MAN

Old blind man, they say you can't see
But every time I walked near, you knew it was me

Your clothes so neat and your tie so straight
Your hair so flawless, you look ready for a political debate.

Old blind man, they say you can't see
You buy your own food and feed your family

Old blind man, your blindness hasn't stopped you
You always seem to know your way
Maybe it's me that's blind, and not you as they say

*The Introduction*

THE WICKED PREVAIL

Sometimes I read in the newspapers or watch on the television; people that are so rich in money, houses and land. It puzzles me how some people have so much and give so little. Surely they can see that they have more money than they can spend.

Why are those people so selfish, mean and greedy? How can they not be conscience of other people that are starving and destitute?

Some people leave their fortunes to pets or useless causes. They would rather throw away food than give it to the poor and the unfortunate.

Why is it that people that feed off of wickedness seem to prevail? Well I believe in my heart that this is only temporary. They can't take their wealth with them when they die. And I truly believe that my wealth may not be here but way beyond the sky.

# THE WICKED PREVAIL

Why? Oh why do the wicked prevail?
Do all my answers lie beyond the veil?

To lift themselves up, they stand on my back
And with every day's beginning, I'm under attack

I work so hard on my job and constantly improve my work
The superiors to me take the credit and make me feel like dirt

Their houses are large and their wealth seems endless
They discredit God and act like they're sinless

They boast of their knowledge and flourish in their greed
They throw away provisions, not caring that others have needs

But I must learn to be patient and stay focused on my goal
All the riches on earth cannot compare to what heaven has to
hold

My weeping today will end in God's tomorrow
The joy that I will have; no man can beg, steal or borrow.

# CHAPTER FOURTEEN

## *DEALING WITH TEENAGERS*

USE YOUR IMAGINATION

I have a teenage daughter the age of sixteen.  I constantly tell her that she can come and talk to me about anything.

I do understand how trying peer pressure can be.  She wants to have friends and become popular in her school.  I have told her that popularity doesn't always come from the things that you do, but sometimes from the things that you don't do.

We are constantly bombarded with sex in songs, videos, television programs and movies.  There seems to be no innocence left in this world.  How do you teach morality without integrating today's lifestyles?

My advice to her was to use her imagination.  Imagine waiting until that special someone comes along.  Imagine how good it would be to have a close friend.  Imagine being in love before making love.

## USE YOUR IMAGINATION

Some say they got to have it even before they know your name
Some think they really need it just to fulfill a foolish game

You need love and devotion, just to make sure of your emotions
Before you open your heart, and before the loving starts

Take your time and follow your mind
Use what you got to get all you need

Use your imagination, you got to find out what love really means
Use your imagination, things are not hard, as they sometimes
seem

Take your time.  Look within
You don't need to pretend
Don't give up; don't give in
Take your time; you can win

Take your time; make it right
It doesn't have to be tonight

Use your imagination

# CHAPTER FIFTEEN

## *ACCOUNTABILITY*

WE NEED PEACE

Our history tells us that since the beginning of man's time, there have been wars.  It tells us that the fighting was over land and religion.  Today the fighting is mostly over oil, gold and other commodities that are prevalent in some regions such as the Middle East and Africa.

The cries for peace fall on deaf ears and the need for love is falling on hardened hearts.  These are huge mountains that some of us are chipping away little by little.  All we can do is stand by our convictions and pray that someday others will realize this as well.

As for religion, I choose to trust and believe in God.
And I will respect others for their beliefs.

*The Poem*

## WE NEED PEACE

In a vision on a desert, walking through the sand
I heard voices from a distance, from a far off land

We need peace, why can't you give us peace?
Love; why can't you give us love?

Time in motion; without a notion. Wasting lives away
Unsung heroes sing a message; 'let's start a brand new day.'

All that we need is for heaven above
To open its gates and rain down love

Take our fellow man and shake him by the hand
Spread love where we can
Because we need a new plan

We need peace

## *The Introduction*

YOU LET PEOPLE SUFFER

I wish that I had one penny for every time I heard someone ask, "Why does God make people suffer?  How can God let these children starve to death?"
Well the truth is that God doesn't starve children; we do!

With all the wealth in the world, how is it that we cannot help feed our fellowman? How does Africa explain the gold and oil that they possess and have children drinking contaminated water?  How can we justify the homeless and hopeless in the world?

I have read that if the top 1000 wealthiest people of the world would donate a small portion of their wealth, no one would be without.

We constantly see commercials for saving the tigers, donkeys, snakes or what have you.  What about people? We are not here to serve animals or the earth; we need to help people first.

Yet hundreds of thousand charities have formed to provide for the needy but less than 20% of the funds actually reach the people.

So stop blaming God for the unfortunate plight of others. Because of your greed and selfishness, you let people suffer!

## YOU LET PEOPLE SUFFER

So many times the question is asked, why does God let people
suffer?

So many times the question is asked, why does God let people
starve?

So many times the question is asked, why does God allow
innocent people to be unjustly punished?

The answer is you
You hoard riches and share with no one

The answer is you
You fill your greedy bodies and discard the extra when you are
done

The answer is you
You have been blessed with more than enough but you still don't
care
The answer is you
You don't give any thanks nor say one single prayer

You live in your big house and drive a new car
When those in need are not very far

The answer is you
With your greed and selfishness
The answer is you
You ignore when your neighbor is in distress

God doesn't make people suffer pain
It is you starting from Abel and Caine.

# CHAPTER SIXTEEN

## *EVERYDAY LIFE'S TRIALS*

JUST ONE OF THOSE DAYS

I am sure that everyone has had one of those days when nothing goes right.  Everything is wrong from the moment you wake up.  The sad thing is that we don't realize this until most of the day has gone.

I don't feel bad about those days because it makes me appreciate the days when things go right.

## JUST ONE OF THOSE DAYS

Another morning, I thought I heard the alarm
Just a few minutes sleep can't do any harm

One hour later
I wake in a daze
And I realized it's going to be just one of those days

Jump into the shower
There's no hot water
My body is cold and the heating is out of order

I dress for work
I can't be late
One more time could just be my fate

Only have time for a glass of orange drink
I'll make it on time; at least I think

I run to the bus stop
It's on time always
Twenty minutes later, it's going to be…just one of those days

I get to the job
The doors are locked shut
I get a bad feeling in the pit of my gut

What will happen to my job and all the bills it pays?
It's going to be just one of those days…It's Saturday!

STRUGGLES

It seems that the only mail that I ever get are bills, notices and fines.  Sometimes I don't know how I cope.  But somehow I am able to pull through those dilemmas.

I work so hard to live from payday to payday.  My life is a never-ending cycle of dread.  My dreams always remain dreams and never turn into reality.  Everyone is available to give advice, but no one is around to give help.

I must always remember that things are not as bad as they could be.  I have food, shelter, clothing and my life, health and strength.  So when I sit and examine and compare my life to others, the struggles aren't really that bad.

**STRUGGLES**

Why, oh why are my struggles so great
Is this anguish just my fate?

I put my heart and soul into every endeavor
Yet the results of my toils tell me never

With every door that closes to me, I shudder
But not one complaint from me, I dare not mutter

As I look the world over and others that suffer
This earthquake of mine is small, as God has been a buffer

To see how much I have been blessed from the eyes of others
I feel ashamed that my cross has been light compared to my
sisters and brothers.

So I will struggle on if I must to the end
I will trust in the Lord knowing that his love will never bend

GOING THROUGH THE FIRE

Once clay has dried, it cannot be changed, re-sculptured or improved upon until it has again been in the fire.  This will make the clay softer and remolding possible.

If you try and relate this to your life, you will understand and be very enlightened.

## GOING THROUGH THE FIRE

I am going through the fire
Not the fire that glows
Not the fire that everyone knows

I am going through the fire of maturity
The pains and groans that are only for me

I have settled into a hard piece of clay
And the fire for me is the only way

I need to be molded all over again
I don't know how long or when

Only in the fire can I be changed
Only in the fire I can be rearranged

Going through the fire are the trials and tribulations
It'll make me appreciative and have more humiliation

I know that God cares for me and all that I aspire
And he knows when I'm strong enough…to go through the fire

GOING THROUGH HELL TO GET TO HEAVEN

When I was young, I would sit on the porch with my grandmother.  We had matching rocking chairs; only mine was smaller.  We would talk about anything and nothing was taboo.  We'd talk about God, being a good person and even sex.

She told me that throughout my life, I would never have true friends; just associates.  She did her best to prepare me for life's journey and to know that I would have to go it alone.

She made sure that I understood that nothing good ever comes easy.  And her favorite saying was "No Cross, No Crown".  I didn't understand it then, but I got it now.

**Going Through Hell to Get To Heaven**

My Grandmother always told me since I was very young
That one of these days, the world would be done

I heard her pray each and every night
That she wanted to be ready and her soul to be right

One thing she did not tell me and I would have to learn
That a place up there, I would have to earn

She did not say that life would be easy
She did not say that there were things that would not please me

She did not tell me about how others would treat me
She did not tell me just how mean people could be

She did not say that there would be times that I would cry
She did not prepare me for the day that she would die.

I feel so alone as the world treads on me
But it is clear to me now, the things that I did not see

Now I am grown and no longer the age of seven
I know that I will have to go through hell…To get to heaven

Made in the USA
Monee, IL
07 July 2026